I0505775

Social Media Bible : Social Media Marketing Strategy Sucessfully for Beginners

Facebook Marketing, Twitter, Google Plus
Advertising : Social Networking Strategy For
Business

By Sanjana Koul

Published By:

Sanjana Koul

© Copyright 2015 – Sanjana Koul

ISBN-13: 978-1507822852
ISBN-10: 1507822855

Table of Contents

Chapter 1:
What Is Social Media
Marketing?

To define the term Social Media Marketing let's first analyze the definition of each word that makes up the term itself. The word 'social' implies that communication is happening between two parties and the term 'media' is simply the platform or method by which people are 'doing' social. And 'marketing' is the act of promoting products and services that lead to sales opportunities.

To summarize, Social Media Marketing is the process of promoting people, brands, products or services using Social Media platforms such as Facebook, Twitter, YouTube, LinkedIn.

While the principles of marketing remain, the strategies and psychology of marketing on each platform can be vastly different. From a business perspective, each Social Media website serves one or more purposes as a marketing medium, the use of which depends on the target market you wish to communicate with (and sell to).

Chapter 2:
Points To Remember Before Engaging Into Social Media Marketing

Define Your Base Strategy

- Setup a budgeted roadmap with intermediate white stones that will help at fine tuning the campaign all along the way. The roadmap should stay in tune with what is being done or what has been done in the real-world. Social Media Marketing is never an innocent act. It is time-consuming and will incur expenses. Being precise about the campaign will definitely decrease the burden. For example, you may need to totally revamp your actual website so as to allow SM integration and SMO. Make your campaign stay SMARRT - Specific, Measurable, Attainable, Realistic, Relevant and Time-bound. Either go for Awareness or Sales or Loyalty. One at a time!

- Don't try to aim for all objectives in one go. Remember! Stick to your company's marketing and communication policy.

Assess And Understand Your Campaign's Environment.

- RESEARCH and don't stop til' you get enough! One surely doesn't want to jump into dark waters without basic precautions and headlamps. So do you with your Social Media Marketing Campaign. Diving irresponsibly into Social Media can spell TOTAL MESS especially when dealing with building awareness and product reputation. Building an effective Online Social Strategy implies thorough knowledge of the competitors' doing's on common platforms (of course)... but above all, take an humble preview of how others from different sectors have done or are doing. Get into both successful and failed case studies. Learn more about technical potentials of each and every Social Network and platform.

Identify These Platforms And Toolsets That Are Relevant And Positively Responsive For Your Roadmap.

- Social Media Marketing is about delivering the same consistent message through the whole spectrum of interwoven Social Networks. The intertwined winning triumvirate is made of the Blog, Facebook and Twitter, to which you would add a YouTube account if you would have video clips uploaded on a regular basis. Choose strategically. For example, you might feel the need of Slideshare and LinkedIn accounts instead of a Foursquare one, if your product or service is more into pitch-intensive B2B.

Realistically Budget And Size Your Online Advertising.

Use the full potential of Google AdSense and Facebook's advertising platforms, but make sure to target wisely. Goal-tied Marketing Campaigns mean nothing without proper advertising. Intuitive Online advertising is now accessible through a few clicks and will definitely unleash its power to communicate about your brand on a global basis. They can also enhance diffusion to limited zones. Think about identifying and assessing your targets on geographical grounds. This will help at optimizing your online advertisement budget. Choosing PPC or CPC is up to you accordingly to your basic roadmap requirements.

Setup A Social Media Taskforce From Within Your Staff And Look For An Outsider To Operate As A Community Manager

The web never sleeps. Social Media Marketing is a 24/7 perpetual roll-on. As such it is time and resource-consuming. One should never expect to be capable of handling a Social Media Marketing campaign alone, especially if other primary company duties are at stake. Instead, invite some of your staff to engage into social networking on your business's behalf. Be choosy though! Those indulged in such a sensitive and interactive task must write well, be tactful, creative and loyal. Outsider Community Managers are seldom biased and are limited to the sole responsibility of consolidating your taskforce's activities over relevant Social Networks. In any case you should build a team whose main goals and capabilities are to listen, learn and reply in tactful manner.

Prefer Influential Relationships.

Get your team to identify major Bloggers and mainstream Social Media activists who fringe with your zones of interest and industry. This task is one of the hinges of success for your campaign. Getting to talk to Social Media heavyweights is like hiring evangelists when relationships get entrusted. Getting Lady Gaga to like your pair of boots is like tapping straight into a sea of opportunities as wide as 9 million individuals who would just follow Gaga's recommendations. Getting her to buy one would mean immediate success. CAREFUL however! The adverse effect is also proportionally as big as your contact's notoriety. Be sure of what you sell to him or her. A successful Social Media Marketing campaign starts here.

Identify Relevant Measuring And Benchmarking Tools.

They are proof of your campaign's success or need for

fine tuning. For example, the increase in the number of likes on Facebook or followers on Twitter is an indicator of your campaign's health. Getting to know how many times your brand is mentioned across the web and rating these comments help at fine tuning the campaign. You should also be able to keep track of your on-growing relationships and traffic that comes from Social Platforms. Identifying prospects for future opportunities helps at developing better strategies. Beware! At the actual state of affairs, Social Media Metrics can be tricky! In fact you will need a very wide array of results coupled to trending reports to be able to depict the exact snapshot of your on-going campaign.

Identify Offline Components That Will Be Needed To Complement Your Online Social Marketing.

Offline events are powerful conversion tools when geared the proper and relevant way. Offline components may also mean socializing with people off the web, in the real world, offering real-world prizes and gifts, organizing rallies, bar camps, conferences and seminars... etc Determine how these components can enhance your target's brand experience and how they will relevantly fit into your Online Marketing Scheme.

Urge For Quality Relevant Content When Posting Articles, Multimedia And Comments.

Praising your 270hp 1974 red Corvette when you advocate for ecological products on your blog isn't the best of strategies. Be sure to lay editorial rules that will define consistent cross-platform content production both in terms of easy-reading literature and technical specifics. Should an uploaded video be in HD both on YouTube and on Facebook? How long should be an article? Should an article contain a generic common byline for multiple authors or should it bear the actual author's name and on what grounds? One should always define these lines accordingly to the targeted audience.

Urge To Stay HUMAN At Every Stage!

Putting up a Social Media Marketing strategy is about building your brand's Social Media presence where your quality accessible content will be delivering values of your organization. Social Media is about... Socializing first! People are touchy when it comes to attitudes and postures. They don't like to bullied or taken as immature consumers. Being too techy, too commercial, demotes the social experience. Simple language and "real-worldlike" politeness are the bases for the best of approaches. It is sometimes more fruitful to start a discussion that may seem miles away from your product and its campaign objectives. With the will to listen and the power to communicate clearly, high conversion rates are never far ahead.

Chapter 3:
Social Media Marketing Strategy

Identify Business Goals

Every piece of your social media strategy serves the goals you set. You simply can't move forward without knowing what you're working toward.

Look closely at your company's overall needs and decide how you want to use social media to contribute to reaching them.

You'll undoubtedly come up with several personalized goals, but there are a few that all companies should include in their strategy—increasing brand awareness, retaining customers and reducing marketing costs are relevant to everyone.

I suggest you choose two primary goals and two secondary goals to focus on. Having too many goals distracts you and you'll end up achieving none.

Set Marketing Objectives

Goals aren't terribly useful if you don't have specific parameters that define when each is achieved. For example, if one of your primary goals is generating leads and sales, how many leads and sales do you have to generate before you consider that goal a success?

Marketing objectives define how you get from Point A (an unfulfilled goal) to Point B (a successfully fulfilled goal). You can determine your objectives with the S-M-A-R-T approach: Make your objectives specific, measurable, achievable, relevant and time-bound.

Using our previous example, if your goal is to generate leads and sales, a specific marketing objective may be to increase leads by 50%. In order to measure your progress, choose which analytics and tracking tools you need to have in place.

Setting yourself up for failure is never a good idea. If you set an objective of increasing sales by 1,000%, it's doubtful you'll meet it. Choose objectives you can achieve, given the resources you have.

You've taken the time to refine your goals so they're relevant to your company, so extend that same consideration to your objectives. If you want to get support from your C-level executives, ensure your objectives are relevant to the company's overall vision.

Attaching a timeframe to your efforts is imperative. When do you intend to achieve your goal(s)? Next month? By the end of this year?

Your objective of increasing leads by 50% may be specific, measurable, achievable and relevant, but if you don't set a deadline for achieving the goal, your efforts, resources and attention may be pulled in other directions.

Identify Ideal Customers

If a business is suffering from low engagement on their social profiles, it's usually because they don't have an accurate ideal customer profile.

Buyer personas help you define and target the right people, in the right places, at the right times with the right messages.

When you know your target audience's age, occupation, income, interests, pains, problems, obstacles, habits, likes, dislikes, motivations and objections, then it's easier and cheaper to target them on social or any other media.

The more specific you are, the more conversions you're going to get out of every channel you use to promote your business.

Research Competition

When it comes to social media marketing, researching your competition not only keeps you apprised of their activity, it gives you an idea of what's working so you can integrate those successful tactics into your own efforts.

Start by compiling a list of at least 3-5 main competitors. Search which social networks they're using and analyze their content strategy. Look at their number of fans or followers, posting frequency and time of day.

Also pay attention to the type of content they're posting and its context (humorous, promotional, etc.) and how they're responding to their fans.

The most important activity to look at is engagement. Even though page admins are the only ones who can calculate engagement rate on a particular update, you can get a good idea of what they're seeing.

For example, let's say you're looking at a competitor's last 20-30 Facebook updates. Take the total number of engagement activities for those posts and divide it by the page's total number of fans. (Engagement activity includes likes, comments, shares, etc.)

You can use that formula on all of your competitors' social profiles (e.g., on Twitter you can calculate retweets and favorites).

Keep in mind that the calculation is meant to give you a general picture of how the competition is doing so you can compare how you stack up against each other.

Choose Channels And Tactics

Many businesses create accounts on every popular social network without researching which platform will bring the most return. You can avoid wasting your time in the wrong place by using the information from your buyer personas todetermine which platform is best for you.

If your prospects or customers tell you they spend 40% of their online time onFacebook and 20% on Twitter, you know which primary and secondary social networks you should focus on.

When your customers are using a specific network, that's where you need to be—not everywhere else.

Your tactics for each social channel rely on your goals and objectives, as well as the best practices of each platform.

Create A Content Strategy

Content and social media have a symbiotic relationship: Without great content social media is meaningless and without social media nobody will know about your content. Use them together to reach and convert your prospects.There are three main components to any successful social media content strategy: type of content, time of posting and frequency of posting.

The type of content you should post on each social network relies on form and context. Form is how you present that information—text only, images, links, video, etc.Context fits with your company voice and platform trends. Should your content be funny, serious, highly detailed and educational or something else?

There are many studies that give you a specific time when you should post on social media. However, I suggest using those studies as guidelines rather than hard rules. Remember, your audience is unique, so you need to test and figure out the best time for yourself.

Posting frequency is as important as the content you share. You don't want to annoy your fans or followers, do you?

Finding the perfect frequency is crucial because it could mean more engagement for your content or more unlikes and unfollows. Use Facebook Insights to see when your fans are online and engaging with your content.

Allocate Budget And Resources

According to recent data from Google, 30% of respondents say that social media has its own new and distinct budget. Of those respondents, 8.7% say their social media budget is pulled from traditional marketing media (i.e., TV, print and radio).I found it interesting that 2/3 of respondents say they plan to increase their social media budget during the upcoming cycle.To budget for social media marketing, look at the tactics you've chosen to achieve your business goals and objectives.Make a comprehensive list of the tools you need (e.g., social media monitoring, email marketing and CRM), services you'll outsource (e.g., graphic design or video production) and any advertising you'll purchase. Next to each, include the annual projected cost so you can have a high-level view of what you're investing in and how it affects your marketing budget.Many businesses establish their budget first, and then select which tactics fit that budget. I take the opposite approach. I establish a strategy first, and thendetermine the budget that fits that strategy.

If your strategy execution fees exceed your budget estimate, prioritize your tactics according to their ROI timeframe. The tactics with the fastest ROI (e.g., advertising and social referral) take priority because they generate instant profit you can later invest into long-term tactics (fan acquisition, quality content creation or long-term engagement).

Assign Roles

Knowing who's responsible for what increases productivity and avoids confusion and overlapping efforts. Things may be a bit messy in the beginning, but with time team members will know their roles and what daily tasks they're responsible for.

When everyone knows his or her role, it's time to start planning the execution process. You can either plan daily or weekly. I don't advise putting a monthly plan together because lots of things will come up and you may end up wasting time adapting to the new changes.

You can use tools like Basecamp or ActiveCollab to manage your team and assign tasks to each member. These tools save you tons of time and help you stay organized.

Chapter 4:
Facebook Advertising Tips

We're starting off our Facebook Advertising & Marketing Guide with some general tips and tricks for advertising on Facebook. Learn to select your campaign objectives, use various Facebook advertising formats for different needs, control the costs of advertising on Facebook, and more.

Go In With Established Goals.

Do you want more website visits? More Facebook likes? More fan engagement? Each of these metrics has its own value, so choose your main objective before you get started. The Facebook ad type you go with will depend on what you're trying to achieve. Facebook's new advertising scheme guides you to recommend ad formats based on your primary goal.

New To Facebook Advertising And Not Sure Where To Start?

Try starting with the Page Likes objective – you'll build your audience and encourage folks to like your page. More likes make you look popular, which encourages more people to like you in a domino effect – it's a safer alternative to buying followers on social media.

Try Facebook Offers To Capture Attention!

Facebook Offers works similar to the Google Offers Extensions, letting you promote a deal exclusively to Facebook users. Try using an offer to give away an item – maybe an ebook or whitepaper – in exchange for an email address. Or create an offer or discount to be redeemed in your brick and mortar store. It's recommended that you target your first Facebook Offer to just your fans. If it goes over well, then you can widen your net to larger audiences.

Drive Downloads For Your Mobile App.

With nearly half of Facebook activity being conducted on mobile devices, Facebook is a clever option for mobile app developers looking to promote their creation.

Include A Clear And Direct Call To Action.

Include a call action in the body text of your Facebook paid ad to encourage FB users to take your desired action

Use Your Facebook Ads To Highlight Special Deals.

Facebook paid advertising can be used to call attention to your latest deals and sale events.

You Don't Need A Facebook Page To Create A Facebook Ad.

You can create an ad for a website by selecting the Clicks to Website objective or the Website Conversions objective. Be aware though that Facebook ads not connected with a Facebook page will appear exclusively in the right column, not in the News Feed.

Try Activating Sponsored Stories As An Add-On

When someone interacts with your Facebook page, offer, event, etc. the action triggers a post, or "story," that the user's friends may then see in their News Feed. These "stories" are generated naturally but are often buried in the News Feed. Opting for sponsored stories basically means you are paying to increase the likelihood that these stories will be seen. You can opt in or out of sponsored stories in the left column of the ad creator tool.

Customize Your Ad Headline.

When promoting a Facebook page, the automatic setup is for the ad headline to be the same as your page's title. Instead of leaving it as-is, type out your own customized ad headline to make the ad more enticing. Aside from your social media image selection, the headline is one of the main ways your ad will make an impact (or fail to).

FB Ads Can Do More Than You Think.

Using Facebook for advertising can help you promote a page, app, or even an event! Exercise all your options.

Let Others Help With Your Ads.

When you add another administrator to your Facebook ads account, they can stop and edit promotions for your page. To add another admin, go to Ad Manager > Settings > Scroll down to Ad Account Roles > Add a User. The user must either be your friend on Facebook or have their email address be searchable on Facebook. Simply choose their access level and click Add.

Chapter 5:
Tips For Controlling
Facebook Advertising Costs

Selecting A Bidding Option.

You can choose from a number of different bid setups for controlling Facebook advertising costs. You can bid for clicks, impressions, or your desired objective (e.g., Facebook page likes). If you choose the recommended (and selected by default) option of bidding based on your objective, your bid will automatically be set to help you reach your objective, whereas bidding for clicks or impressions allows for more customization.

Choose Between Daily Or Lifetime Budget.

As an advertiser, you can choose to set up a daily budget or a lifetime budget. A daily budget controls how much you will spend on a specific campaign per day. Your ads and sponsored stories stop showing once you hit your daily ad budget, helping your budget Facebook advertising rates based on each daily cycle. Lifetime budget lets you select how much you want to spend over the entire span of time a campaign is scheduled to run. Don't forget that each campaign has a separate budget, so plan accordingly to keep Facebook advertising prices within your comfort zone.

Want To Change You Ad Campaign?

You can edit your campaign's end date or budget anytime after the campaign has started running. While you can't change your minimum daily spend limit (it's set at $50), you can change your daily ad budget, which ultimately is what really controls the cost of Facebook advertising

Chapter 6:
Visual Facebook Advertising Tips

4 Ways to Create More Engaging Image Ads

Images are a powerful tool you can utilize for creating engaging, eye popping Facebook ads. Learn how to make the most of your Facebook image ads.

Go Crazy With The Images!

Posts and Facebook PPC ads with images get much higher engagement than those without, as they help your ad or post stand out from a flooded news feed.

Add Multiple Images To Your Ads.

Add multiple images to a Facebook PPC ad for extra variety and to test how different images coupled with your ad text perform. You can upload up to six images to accompany your ads at no extra cost.

On Image Ads, Keep Text Under 20%.

Facebook advertising rules dictate that image-based Facebook ads that are set to appear in users' news feeds won't get approved if the text takes up more than 20% of the image space. Facebook has a grid tool to help ensure that your image ad follows the guidelines, but as Jon Loomer has noted, sometimes you can get around this simply by moving your text around slightly.

What Size Image Should You Use?

Facebook recommends uploading an image that is 1200x627 pixels for your ads. You'll be provided with more specific image size recommendations depending on the type of ad you're creating, but make sure your image is at least 600 pixels wide for appearing in the News Feed.

Chapter 7:
Advertising With Facebook

Facebook advertising has some incredible targeting capabilities that can help you tailor your message and target your desired audiences. Take full advantage of Facebook advertising targeting options to create highly successful Facebook ad campaigns. Seven Best ways of doing that is discussed below:

Take Advantage Of Advanced Targeting Options

Facebook has a ton of awesome and unique targeting options for FB paid ads you won't find elsewhere. You can target audiences by location, age, gender, workplace, relationship status, language, education and more.

Zone In On Your Ideal Audience With Interest Targeting

In addition to the targeting options mentioned above, Facebook allows for some incredible deep interest targeting. This provides tremendous value, and the interest targeting capabilities alone can justify your use of Facebook advertising.

Make New Friends Or Focus On The Old.

You can target your Facebook ads exclusively to users who are already connected to your Facebook page, or you can choose to target them and their friends, or those who aren't connected to your page yet at all. (Remember that extending your reach may reduce the relevance of your audience and cost a little more.)

Keep An Eye On Your Potential Audience Meter

As you add targeting options and narrow your audience, Facebook will generate an approximate number of people you'll reach. This is only an estimate, but can help you make sure you're not targeting too many people (or too few). Ads perform best when they're targeted to at least a few thousand people, so consider removing some restrictions if your audience is dipping below this.

Narrow Your Target With More Categories.

If you only have a few interests targeted, try adding related topics in the "More Categories" section. There you'll find options for narrowing your audience even further - choose users who have had a birthday recently, who upload a lot of photos on Facebook, etc.

Want To Bring Customers In Store?

Try targeting people who live in your town or local area. Couple this with Facebook Offers to be redeemed in store and see just how much in-store footfall you can get from being social.

Upload Your Mailing List To Facebook.

If you're looking to build upon existing leads, you can add a custom audience and upload your mailing list directly to Facebook, enabling you to target users you have an existing relationship with. Taking advantage of the custom audiences feature often increases ad conversion rates. You can upload a mailing list or connect directly with Mail Chimp. Just click "Create New Audience" in the Audiences section.

Chapter 8:
20 Facebook Marketing Tips: Practically Free Posts & Promotions That Help Your Biz

Host A Contest!

In the past marketers were required to use a third-party application for FB contests, but Facebook recently changed their policy and now allows contests to be hosted directly on Facebook. Hosting a giveaway or contest on Facebook has never been easier!

Hide Valuable Content Behind A Like Barrier

Hiding valuable content behind a like barrier will get more likes to your page – be sure to include a colorful and captivating call to action graphic to seal the deal.

Lights, Camera, Youtube.

Videos have crazy high engagement rates, so use them in

your posts to get some serious attention.

Keep It Short.

Concise posts tend to fare better than their lengthier counterparts – it's recommended that you trim down your words to somewhere between 100 and 250 characters for optimal engagement. No one's looking to read the next great American novel in their News Feed.

Update Your Cover Photo.

Change your Facebook cover to mix things up. Changing a cover photo to reflect a season or time of year shows fans that you are making an effort to be active and stay relevant. Updating your cover photo to advertise a special sale or giveaway will also help those events get more attention than they might receive otherwise.

Post Frequently And Consistently.

Don't worry about overdoing the posts – as long as they are spaced evenly through the day, you'll be fine. Only 16% of your fans will see one post (if even that), as news feeds easily become over populated. The more you post, the better your chances are of being seen. However, do remember to focus on quality over quantity – every post should be of value, not just something thrown quickly together.

Use Facebook Insights To Measure Your Success.

Insights lets you see your most popular and successful posts in terms of link clicks, shares, and likes. This data is extremely valuable and ignoring it is like ignoring conversion tracking for AdWords – it's just plan silly! You should be using this data to see what you're doing right, and then do more of it.

Deliver Shout Outs With Facebook Tagging

Including tags in your posts is a great way to broaden your exposure, especially when working with other organizations. If you run a doggy grooming company and are giving away Petco squeaky toys, tag them with an @Petco. When they see the tag, they'll be more likely to share your post with their fans, multiplying your reach by a ton! There's no reason not to be generous with tags. Tag conferences you're attending, businesses whose articles you're sharing, favorite clients, etc. Everyone likes to get noticed, and they'll remember that you were the one to put them in the limelight.

#Hash It Out

In a similar vein, Facebook has hashtags enabled and you

might as well use them. Hashtags are a great tool for promoting a specific campaign you want to raise awareness of (like our own recent #GradeAndGetPaid). It's a nice way to seamlessly connect Twitter and Facebook marketing efforts. Hashtags also help categorize your posts by topic, and while the popularity of Facebook hashtags isn't exactly skyrocketing, you can search hashtag terms to discover fan conversations you may want to participate in.

Share Testimonials On Facebook.

Testimonials are always powerful, and that rule continues on Facebook. However, it's good to think outside the box when delivering testimonials on a social network. Rather than bland words, incorporate photos, videos, or other media.

Ask Questions!

Facebook users love to get their voices out and feel heard. Try incorporating questions or surveys into your posts for engagement. Keep the questions simple though – no one feels like filling out the SATs on Facebook.

Participate In Fun Themed Posts

Joining in on weekly movements like #ThrowbackThursday or posting about goofy holidays gives you a chance to have fun with fans.

Share Exclusive Content For Facebook Fans.

Posting special, top secret content just for fans on Facebook adds a sense of exclusivity and belonging for your following. Post information or tidbits they might not find elsewhere.

Share Fan-Created Content.

Sharing fan-made content is a great way to bolster a true sense of community among your followers. It shows that you care and makes fans feel valued and appreciated – who doesn't want that?

Fill In The Blanks.

Another strategic post format to drive engagement is the fill in the _____ tactic. Users' eyes are drawn to the _____, and getting eyeballs is half the battle. Make sure to incorporate a large colorful photo for added attention. Track your engagement metrics and see how the post performs!

Photo Captions.

Asking for users to provide a caption to an exciting or laugh-worthy photo is another smart strategy to drive interaction and engagement.

Don't Quote Me On This, But Quotes Rock.

Posts involving inspiring or life-affirming quotes often perform very well. For an added bonus, attach a photo to your quote – even better, do Pinterest-style image/quote overlay. People eat that stuff up!

Jump On The Meme Wagon

Memes work on the same principle as quotes, but with auto meme generators they are easier to create. Folks love 'em though! We create our own PPC memes from time to time and they tend to do well.

Have Users "Vote" With The Like And Share Buttons.

As we've said, people love to express their thoughts and opinions on Facebook. Sometimes they like it too much, but you might as well have those soapbox speakers benefit you! Ask users to choose option A or option B, with a vote for A as a "Like" and a vote for B as a "Share." You'll get some of both and will broaden your post reach and engagement a TON. The more controversial the topic, the more engagement you'll be likely to see.

Chapter 9:
Twitter Marketing Tips

I have discussed below in detail the the essential Twitter Marketing Tips

Improve Your Tweets

(a) Share valuable content in your own voice

Do your best to craft your content tweets, @replies and promotional tweets all with a flawless style that matches your personality and/or brand. Ideally, you want people to read your tweets and feel naturally compelled to click on your links and retweet you.You just want to add value and have no agenda or attachment to "making the sale," yet you're strategic and mindful about how you tweet. Then you'll see a marked improvement in your retweet and click-through rates.

(b) Use keywords in your tweets

Keywords have been and continue to be a relevant and driving force for web content (whether we're talking about a website, blog post, Facebook update or a tweet). Keywords are the backbone of content.So I'd have to say hands-down, my best Twitter marketing tip for business is to make a list of keywords that best describe your business and industry. Use these words as you compose your 140-character posts.Think quality over quantity. Make every character and tweet count!

(c)   Share links to useful content

Sharing links to useful content is, statistically speaking, more effective at growing and retaining followers than "engaging" with them in conversation.That's not to say that conversations aren't useful in helping people to like you, but if you want to grow your fan base, you need toshare more links than you do @replies.

(d) Use search features to discover what your clients want

Use the search feature in a Twitter tool like HootSuite to watch for conversations about a problem your business can solve. It will give you insight into what is on your prospects' minds and provide an open door for you to help them.

Try providing a link to a great article or video that answers their question. This one action could lead to an ongoing dialogue that in turn may lead to a customer relationship later.

(e) Connect with the right people and tweet with them

There are two crucial things businesses should focus on when implementing their Twitter strategy.

The first is not finding just anyone to follow in hopes

36

that they follow you back, but finding relevant people to follow who are more likely to follow you back. You can bloat your account to 100,000+ followers, but if they are not interested in your content, it gets you nowhere. You need to be using tools such as Follower Wonk, Twellow and Wefollow to find people who are in your region (if you're a local business) and interested in your industry. Then start following them.

The second is after you find your targeted audience, don't just tweet at them—tweet with them. Follow their conversations; add in your two cents from time to time. Follow anyone who talks about your brand and thank them for their compliments or help them with their concerns. Follow anyone who talks about your industry and show why you are an authority.

Doing these things will help you run a successful Twitter campaign that will give your brand exposure as a leader in your industry!

(f) Use a classic icebreaker

Most followers become nameless, faceless numbers on a follower list. Remember when networking used to be about meeting people face to face? Icebreakers were important then, and they're just as important now in the virtual world.

Icebreakers help you share a common connection with a stranger—and make you memorable enough to begin and sustain a long-term relationship.

When you find relevant tweets from among your

followers, retweet their blog link—and follow the author's feed. Then send them an @message, detailing something insightful about their blog post. At the end of the tweet, link to a similar post you've written.

This should result in more blog comments, retweets and followers, all from 10 minutes of effort. Twitter is all about icebreakers, and collecting followers who instantly recognize you in a sea of faces. Invest time in your introductions and they'll make all the difference to your feed.

(g) Cultivate relationships

Pay attention when someone tweets about your blog posts or retweets something you've shared. When you are building a business, never take it for granted when people help you spread the word. Start by thanking them for the tweet. And take it a step further: add them to a private list for tweeters and retweeters.

At least once every day for five minutes, review the tweets in that list. Look for great content that you might have missed, information from smart people you need to follow and conversation trends you might have missed. Jump into conversations, retweet items your community would appreciate and thank people for sharing great things.

But most of all, get to know more about these people who volunteered to become part of your team by sharing your content. It's all about relationships, and Twitter helps you build relationships with these important members of your community.

(h) Engage your audience

Find ways to reach out and engage your audience. Too many businesses want to just set their Twitter feed on autopilot or constantly push promotional content.

Although there is a place for the promotional tweet, your feed will receive much more attention if you make it a resource for your followers. Sharing articles of interest, leading discussions on topics important to your industry, answering questions and sometimes just being there can do this.

It's about creating relationships and building trust in those relationships. Although they may not be clients now, when the time comes, you've already cleared the first hurdle for your followers.

(i) Be helpful

Plenty of people are filling up Twitter streams with the tech-equivalent of screaming infomercials to buy things. Effective marketing on Twitter takes time. But it also takes more than just selling or pushing your message.

Engaging and interacting with your consumers in a consistent and helpful way will keep your product or service at top of mind. Not everyone needs your offering right now. You want to provide information and solutions that keep them reading, so when they need what you have, they know you're there for them.

(j) Transparency lends credibility

If you mess up, admit it. If you don't know the answer to a question, admit it. If you're inexperienced, admit it. If you're willing to admit that your business is not perfect and is a work-in-progress or open to suggestion, your audience is more likely to take you seriously. You build your company's credibility and trustworthiness.

The quickest way to lose credibility? If, as a business, you attempt to cover-up, lie or over-promise and under-deliver.

Bring Twitter Followers Back To Your Website

(k) Use hashtags to create and curate conversations around your brand

You can reward your followers when they participate by retweeting them or displaying their tweets on your site or blog.

Bergdorf Goodman is a high-end clothing and shoe retailer that is using the Instagram photo app as well as a Twitter hashtag (#BGShoes) to encourage fans to tweet pictures of their shoes (purchased at BG of course) around the city of New York.

Here's another example, the San Francisco Food Bank (@SFFoodBank) gave followers a challenge: Try to spend less than $5/day on food. And tweet about it along the way, using the #hungerchallenge hashtag.

Participants are listed on the Hunger Challenge website (and you can pity them in real time as they tweet about their barely full bellies, all captured in the hash tag stream: http://twitter.com/#!/search/hungerchallenge).

(l) Share links back to your website for list-building

In most cases, people aren't going to buy from you right off of a site like Twitter. You need to shift your thinking from "How can I get this person to buy from me or hire me now?" to "How can I bring this person into my community and strengthen the relationship with him/her on an ongoing basis?"

One of the best ways to do this is to encourage visits to your blog or website by providing something of value for free in exchange for email addresses. (Make sure what you're giving them is extra-juicy and useful!) That way, you have permission to keep in touch and build an ongoing relationship with prospects.

This shouldn't be thought of as list-building just for the sake of boosting your subscriber numbers; rather, it's a natural continuation of the solid foundation you've begun building with a potential client or customer within the Twitterverse.

(m) Tweet links to your blog more often

When you're thinking about using social media for lead generation, you want to use Twitter as not only a conversation channel, but also as a way to drive traffic to your content. I found a significant increase in traffic from Twitter and engagement with our account when I posted several tweets of a blog post rather than one the morning. It gives your followers a chance to catch that link if they missed it the first time and also targets people in different time zones.

Don't be spammy and go overboard, but sharing your content several times (if it's valuable) will give you the extra edge.

(n) Connect your LinkedIn account with your Twitter account

Syncing your LinkedIn account with your Twitter account can make your Twitter activities much more relevant to business. Not only can you share content across both networks simultaneously, but also you can keep track of your professional connections from LinkedIn and follow their tweets!

Here are three tips:

- Make sure to add your Twitter account to your LinkedIn profile. Visitors to your profile will be able to follow you on Twitter right there from your profile page! Have more than one Twitter account (perhaps personal and business)? Add them both to your LinkedIn profile and designate your primary account.

- Install the LinkedIn "Tweets" application on your LinkedIn profile and immediately go through and follow each of your LinkedIn connections who have

Twitter profiles. In most cases, your professional connections are going to follow you back!

- Create a Twitter list of your LinkedIn connections automatically with the click of a button using the Twitter applic ation in LinkedIn. This makes it easy to follow the stream of updates on Twitter coming from your professional connections.
- Twitter is a firehose of information, data and resources. I'm a big fan of making sense out of that data and making it more relevant to your professional network! Integrating your Twitter account with LinkedIn profile

(o) Make Twitter Tools Work for You

Take advantage of tools to help curate and share relevant content

Sending out 140-character messages every so often may not seem like a task that requires marketing automation software but, to the contrary, these tools can greatly improve the effectiveness of your Twitter marketing.

There are a slew of services available, some free and some paid, to help manage your Twitter account. At Strutta, we use the HootSuite dashboard to track Twitter activity, which can be easily categorized into multiple streams that we follow.

We also use Summify to help filter through the noise and surface news that is most relevant to our industry. This enables us to find content that is both useful to consume and valuable to share with our followers via retweeting. Sharing relevant content from other trusted sources helps establish your credibility, especially when mixed with your own original content.

(p) Add columns of searches in HootSuite

I have a separate tab in HootSuite set up only for searches that I want to monitor throughout the day. I have several columns of searches on this tab so I can see in one glance what people are talking about with respect to those searches at any given moment.

I use a combination of searching on hashtags and searching on just keywords.

Then I also have a search where I put the words "how do I" which will give me an exact match on that phrase, and the word "Facebook" which will show both of those key phrases anywhere within the tweet.

I'm looking for people asking questions about Facebook that I can help with. I can then answer the person's question and perhaps follow them. When you help people who have questions about your niche on Twitter, you stand out as a leader and authority in your field.

Make sure you are authentically helping people out and not giving a sales pitch. So if you want to watch for people asking questions about your niche—which is yoga, for example—you would put the keywords "how do I" and "yoga." Or you may find that a better search question could be "where do I." Test out different keyword phrases to see what works best for your business.

(q) Get a Twitter tutorial from your teenager

I was at a conference last week where a professor who specializes in new and emerging media made this confession—he frequently asks his students to teach him how to use Twitter, Facebook, LinkedIn and other social media tools.

He went on to explain that at one point, during one of his tutorials, a student turned to him and said, "Aren't I paying YOU to teach me this stuff?"

The truth is, if you're like most businesspeople, it's very hard to keep up with all of the changes taking place. One way to get more efficient about using Twitter and other tools is to sit down with someone younger than you and ask him or her for a front-lines tutorial.

Oh sure, we all understand the CONCEPT of Twitter, but when it comes to the practical application or the unwritten rules, it's hard to keep up. The solution, I've found, is to not be shy about asking someone younger for a brief, in-the-trenches tutorial. In the long run, it'll save you hours and hours of anguish.

Chapter 10: Marketing Strategy For Google Plus

Following are 13 "Google Plus Tools" which can help you to improve your marketing:

Take Advantage Of The Youtube Integration

If you have a YouTube channel but haven't taken advantage of its relationship with Google+, you need to. Whether you've already established yourself on YouTube (or Google+), you'll reach a wider audience when you use them in conjunction. Take advantage of the integration! For example, when you share a YouTube video to Google+, users can view the video within Google+. Any comments on that Google+ share show up as comments on your YouTube video.

Increase Your Reach

Webinars are a powerful tool for building email lists and a loyal audience. Unfortunately, webinar software can be clunky and expensive. Google+ has an easy alternative. Hangouts On Air provides a free video broadcasting service that lets you stream a live feed to your YouTube channel for recording, and of course is completely integrated with Google+.

Why is it important to use? According to Stephan Hovnanian, using Hangouts On Air drastically increases your brand's reach.

If you're looking to build your own Hangouts On Air audience, I recommend visiting HOAShows and submitting your hangout to the directory. HOAShows is one of the more robust and regularly updated Hangouts On Air directories. (It's also a great place to find other great Hangouts On Air.)

Keep The Conversation Going

With Google Drive, Google's cloud-based file management and storage service, you can share an incredible amount of information with your Google+ audience, including presentation slideshows, PDFs and even password-protected documents.

These supplemental documents (e.g., worksheets and notes with key takeaways) add significant value to your Hangouts On Air and can keep the conversation going after your event.

Store Your Pictures

How are you backing up the pictures from your phone? Did you know you can use Google+ to store your pictures for safekeeping? Google+ is a reliable way to store your pictures, and then delete them from your phone.Once uploaded, you can highlight the important pictures, enhance them so they look better or create image galleries—and easily share all of them.

Extend The Life Of Your Content

Google+ Embedded Posts is a cool feature that lets you share your Google+ posts on your blog.

The benefits of embedded posts are twofold. First, post content created within Google+ is eventually lost within the news stream. Embedding that same post on your blog extends the life of the content.

Second, Google+ content embedded on your blog is directly tied to your Google+ profile. If your readers are logged into their Google+ accounts, any +1s, shares or comments show on both your blog and your Google+ content.

In the example below, HubSpot embedded a Google+ post on their blog. The embedded post records +1s and shares just as if the user was on Google+ instead of the website.

Create Animated Videos With Photos

Videos are popular because they're visually attractive and (usually) a quick way to consume content.

Google+'s Auto   Awesome feature   lets   you create

animated videos with photos, videos or both. It's a really cool effect and has endless possibilities for video-minded marketers.

To create your video using Auto Awesome on Google+, you'll need to download the Google+ app for your smartphone and make sure you have the correct settings enabled. Go into Settings > Camera Settings and turn on Auto Backup, Auto Awesome and Auto Enhance.

After taking your pictures, upload them to Google+, then wait a few minutes and check your photo album. Google will automatically make the video.

Take Full Advantage Of Images

Visual content is the best way to catch your audience's attention. Wouldn't it be great if all social networks agreed to use the same dimensions for shared images? As it stands, we're stuck formatting images to match the various dimensions for Twitter, Instagram and Facebook.

The truth is, not every image we want to share fits within each restricted space. We're forced to do one of three things to share images across platforms: crop or resize the image, share it and have it look odd or not share the image at all. None are ideal outcomes.

Google+ is different. It doesn't auto-crop your images or require you to resize them before posting.

Format Your Posts

Readers want to consume as much information as they can in as little time as possible. Scannable content is a must if you want any social media marketing success at all.

LinkedIn, Twitter and Facebook don't let you format your post content. That means you can't always draw your reader's eye to the important parts of your post (e.g., links or media you're promoting).

Google+, on the other hand, allows you to add simple variables such as "*" for bold and "_" for italics to quickly grab your readers' attention.

Use Relevant Hashtags

Just like Twitter and Instagram (and unlike Facebook), hashtags can have a notable impact on reaching a targeted audience on Google+. The Explore feature uses hashtags to help Google+ users quickly find and interact with topics they're interested in.

When you create sharable content, check Explore to see how your topic relates to trending hashtags and use them if they apply. Or if you see a hashtag relevant to your brand or industry, create content around that topic and share it (including the hashtag, of course).

Soundcloud

No media empire is complete without its own broadcasting network. Google+ has integrated SoundCloud, the audio platform that enables sound creators to upload, record, promote and share their originally created sounds.

This means you can share files from SoundCloud and play them from within a Google+ post. Now your audience can consume, comment and share your audio content without having to leave Google+. It's just one more way to increase your content's reach.

Segment Your Audience

Google+ circles are one of the most important tools of Google+. Unlike other social networks, circles are much more than "people who see your content." They're more like subscribers.

As you connect with other Google+ members (or they connect with you), you can place them in circles, which are essentially lists that let you easily segment contacts.

When Google+ connections give you permission (and make no mistake, permission isvery important) to contact them, you can directly notify them via circles. To distribute permission-based, targeted traffic to your posts, just include "circle" in the to:field of your post shares.

I want to make a comment about proper Google+

etiquette. While this type of contact is similar to the way you contact email subscribers, it's important note that you should never notify your Google+ connections via email. Their permission to contact them only extends to Google+.

Use +Post Ads

+Post ads take Google+ posts and create display ads that run across Google's ad network of over two million web properties. According to Google, +post ads are way to "amplify your content and create conversations across the web."

This is a revolutionary concept for marketers from many standpoints, but most notably the direction of engagement.

Twitter and Facebook ads run inside their respective social networks and work to push consumers to outside websites—away from the network.

Google +post ads run outside of the network and work to pull consumers back to Google+. +Post Ads let people comment, join a hangout, +1 or follow your brand right from within the ad.

Track In-Depth Analytics

Marketers have to track social media marketing efforts and the key performance indicators (KPIs) attached to them.

You can find many analytics tools that integrate with Google+, but here are my recommendations (all either free or with quality free options): SumAll, CircleCount and Steady Demand.

SumAll analyzes more than just Google+, and marketers will enjoy the visual representation of published posts, post engagement and new Google+ followers.

CircleCount was one of the first tools to track activity within Google+. It has continued to be a valuable tool because it provides a database of influencers, allowing you to make important connections.

Steady Demand's Google+ Brand Page Audit tool is a good option for Google+ pages. This free tool quickly analyzes your Google+ brand page to make sure you've properly set up all of the basic functionality Google+ brand pages have to offer.